POCAHONTAS

Troll Associates

POCAHONTAS

by Laurence Santrey

Illustrated by David Wenzel

Troll Associates

Library of Congress Cataloging in Publication Data

Santrey, Laurence.
   Pocahontas.

   Summary: A biography of the seventeenth-century Indian
princess whose friendship toward the English settlers
at Jamestown was a key factor in making the colony a
success.
    1. Pocahontas, d. 1617—Juvenile literature.
2. Powhatan Indians—Biography—Juvenile literature.
3. Jamestown (Va.)—History—Juvenile literature.
4. Virginia—History—Colonial period, ca. 1600-1775—
Juvenile literature. [1. Pocahontas, d. 1617.
2. Powhatan Indians—Biography. 3. Indians of North
America—Biography. 4. Virginia—History—Colonial
period, ca. 1600-1775] I. Wenzel, David, 1950-   ill.
II. Title.
E99.P85P578   1985   975.5'01'0924 [B]   84-8443
ISBN 0-8167-0276-4 (lib. bdg.)
ISBN 0-8167-0277-2 (pbk.)

The Indian princess, Pocahontas, was the daughter of Powhatan, the powerful chief of a tribe of Eastern Woodlands Indians. Pocahontas played a major role in aiding the English settlers in the New World. Without her help, the colony of Jamestown in Virginia might have perished in its first years of existence.

Although the exact date of her birth is not known, Pocahontas was probably born in 1595. This date is based on the fact that she looked about twelve years old in 1607, when the colonists first arrived in Virginia. They also described her as playful, athletic, and very intelligent.

From the very beginning, the Indian girl was fascinated by the newcomers to her land. Almost every day, Pocahontas visited the small settlement at Jamestown. She carefully observed how the settlers built their houses, dressed, prepared their food, and acted toward one another. And she was eager to learn their language so she could talk to them.

One of Pocahontas's first friends in the settlement was the soldier Captain John Smith. Captain Smith taught her many words in English. In turn, she taught him the language of the Powhatan Indians.

Pocahontas was a good teacher, because Captain Smith was soon able to use her language with ease. Pocahontas was an equally good student, who learned the English language and customs quickly and well.

The young Indian girl saw that the James-town colonists were having many problems. Most of the colonists were finely dressed and well spoken. But they lacked the skills needed to survive in the wilderness. They simply did not know how to farm or fish in the new land, how to clear the land, or how to build on it. That is because the majority of the colonists were gentlemen, raised to have work done for them.

The Jamestown colonists had sailed to the New World to establish an English colony and to discover a northwest sea route to the Far East. They also hoped to find gold. Instead, they found hard times, sickness, and hostile Indians.

A total of about one hundred colonists had landed in the New World in the spring of 1607. By the end of that summer, many had died. For the rest, the prospects of surviving the winter were extremely poor.

But Pocahontas helped to save the colony. That fall, when she saw that the settlers were almost out of food and had failed to store provisions for the coming winter, she immediately spoke to her people. She convinced the Indians to give some of their corn to the English. And she persuaded her half brother, Pochins, to bring fish to Jamestown.

Then Pocahontas talked to the Indians of a nearby village, and they agreed to share their wild game with the settlers. This was the Indian girl's way of repaying the friendship shown her by Captain Smith. As Smith later wrote, "Pocahontas was the instrument to preserve this colony from death, famine, and utter confusion."

Although Pocahontas was always friendly to the Jamestown colonists, this was not true of most of the Indians in the area. They were frightened of the rifles carried by the newcomers. And they were worried that more foreigners would come to take away their lands.

Moreover, the people of one tribe were usually hostile to any other tribe that tried to move into their territory. So they were treating the Jamestown colonists the same way. Beyond that, however, part of the trouble was caused by the behavior of the colonists.

To many of the settlers, the Indians were nothing more than savages. Sometimes the colonists would arrange to trade with the Indians in return for food. But many times the colonists did not bargain fairly. This only served to increase the hostility the Indians felt for the newcomers to their land. These bad feelings led to the capture of

Captain John Smith in December 1607. Smith had taken a small party of men to explore the Chickahominy River. They were hoping to find a way of getting to the other side of America, and from there to the Far East. They had no idea that the Pacific Ocean was more than three thousand miles away.

The party traveled upriver as far as their boat could take them. Then Captain Smith, with two other colonists and two Powhatan Indian guides, continued the trip in a dugout canoe.

When they could go no farther by water, the party beached the canoe. Two of the colonists and one Indian were left to make a temporary camp. Smith and the other Indian went off to explore the surrounding woods.

Not long after, Captain Smith found himself trapped by a large number of Powhatan Indians, armed with bows and arrows. The Indian guides had tricked him and his men.

Smith was taken back to the temporary campsite, where he discovered that his fellow colonists had been killed. Smith feared that his fate would be the same.

The Indians marched the English soldier many miles through the forest, until they reached a village. The chief of the village was Opechancanough, who was a brother of

Pocahontas's father, Powhatan. Opechancanough was a fierce, merciless warrior who
wanted to destroy the entire Jamestown
colony.

He promised to set Smith free and give him many presents if the captain would tell him how to successfully attack the fort. Smith refused to betray Jamestown, even if it cost him his life.

Captain Smith was then taken to the village of the great chief, Powhatan. The Englishman was to be executed there. A mound of stones was built in the center of the village. Captain Smith was dragged to the mound, and his head was forced down onto the stones. A powerful warrior stood nearby, ready to execute Smith.

Suddenly, Pocahontas ran forward and placed her head on top of Captain Smith's head. She begged her father to spare his life. At first, Powhatan was upset that his daughter had interrupted the important ceremony. But he could not deny her request. It was a tribal custom that a woman could adopt a condemned prisoner, thereby saving the life of that prisoner.

Pocahontas was now the guardian of her friend, Captain John Smith. To show that he accepted this arrangement, Powhatan adopted Captain Smith as his son and gave him the name "Nantaquoud." Soon afterward, Smith was allowed to return to Jamestown.

For the next two years, the relationship between the colonists and the Indians varied. There were periods of peace and periods of conflict. But through the good times and bad times, Pocahontas remained a friend, bringing food to Jamestown. She didn't stop visiting the fort until 1609, when Captain Smith returned to England.

Four years later, in 1613, Pocahontas was captured by a group of colonists. They took the eighteen-year-old princess to Jamestown. Word was sent to Chief Powhatan that his daughter would be returned if he would free some prisoners he had taken, and return the tools and guns that had been taken with these prisoners. Powhatan sent back the prisoners but kept the tools and guns. The English retaliated by refusing to release Pocahontas.

While Pocahontas was a hostage, she was converted to Christianity. Her new name was Rebecca. During this time, she met John Rolfe, a wealthy Englishman. They fell in love and were married in April 1614.

Chief Powhatan did not attend the wedding. He did, however, send a splendid necklace of freshwater pearls to Pocahontas. And he gave the newlyweds a large tract of land on the James River. The Rolfes lived on this land for the next two years. It was there that their son, Thomas, was born.

In 1616, Pocahontas sailed for England with her husband and child. The Indian princess was an immediate sensation in England. She was received at court by the king and queen, and admired wherever she went. Her English was excellent, her manners perfect, and her intelligence clearly superior. She came as quite a surprise to the many people who thought all Indians were "uncivilized."

The high point of Pocahontas's visit to England occurred when she once again saw Captain John Smith. For years she had believed he was dead, and the sight of him overwhelmed her.

Captain Smith was equally delighted to see his Indian friend. They spoke for many hours, learning what had happened to each other in the years that had passed.

Pocahontas . Aº 1616

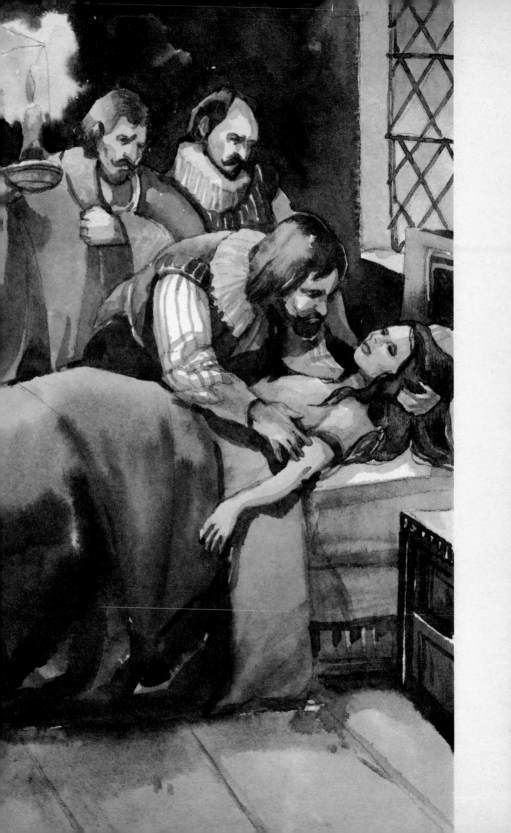

Although Pocahontas enjoyed her time in England, she was not well. Her health grew steadily worse during the winter of 1616. But she looked forward to returning home in the spring. Pocahontas was sure her health would improve once she was back home.

The Rolfes were planning to sail for Virginia in March of 1617, aboard a ship named the *George*. They were staying at Gravesend, waiting to board the ship, when Pocahontas became deathly ill. Some historians believe she had smallpox. Others believe it was either pneumonia or tuberculosis. Whatever the illness may have been, it took her life on March 21, 1617.

Pocahontas was buried in Gravesend, at St. George's Parish Church. Her life had been short, but in that lifetime, Pocahontas did much to bring success to the early settlers of the New World.